EQUILIBRIUM

D1027943

Winner of the 2016 Frost Place Chapbook Competition

EQUILIBRIUM

poems by

TIANA CLARK

DURHAM, NORTH CAROLINA

EQUILIBRIUM

Winner of the 2016 Frost Place Chapbook Competition
Selected by Afaa Michael Weaver

Published in the United States of America

Library of Congress Cataloging-in-Publication Data

Clark, Tiana
Equilibrium: poems / by Tiana Clark
p. cm.
ISBN-13: 978-1-4951-5764-6

Cover design: Victoria Lynne McCoy
Book design: F. H. Spock Studio

Cover image:
Amy Sherald
Equilibrium, 2012
Oil on canvas
100 x 67 inches
Collection of the United States Embassy Dakar, Senegal
Courtesy the artist and Monique Meloche Gallery, Chicago

Published by
BULL CITY PRESS
1217 Odyssey Drive
Durham, NC 27713

www.BullCityPress.com

ACKNOWLEDGMENTS

The author would like to thank the editors of the following journals, in which these poems first appeared:

The Adroit Journal: "A Psalm for The One"
Best New Poets 2015: "The Frequency of Goodnight"
Crab Orchard Review: "Particle Fever"
HEArt Online: "Hair Relaxer: an Origin Story"
Muzzle Magazine: "Broken Ghazal for Walter Scott,"
                    "How to Find the Center of a Circle"
The Offing: "BNA → LAX"
Rattle: "Equilibrium," "Exorcism," "Sandy Speaks"
Southern Indiana Review: "A Blue Note for Father's Day"
Tinderbox Poetry Journal: "The Spot in Antioch"
Thrush Poetry Journal: "Bear Witness"
Word Riot: "Magic"

"Magic" also appeared in *Native Magazine*

Thanks to the Board of Trustees of The Frost Place, the Creative Writing Program at Vanderbilt University, the New Harmony Writers Workshop, the Porch Writers' Collective, Metropolitan Nashville Arts Commission, and the Schomburg Center for Research in Black Culture for their generous support and funding.

Many thanks to Afaa Michael Weaver, Ross White, Kendra DeColo, Kate Daniels, Mark Jarman, Rick Hilles, Beth Bachmann, Jeff Hardin, Ross Gay, Ciona Rouse, Leslie LaChance, Patricia Alice Albrecht, Chance Chambers, Walker Bass, Poetry in the Brew crew, LCC, Allison Inman (Elizabeth T. and Margy), Joyce Sohl and Scarritt Bennett Center, DD, Linds, Dan Haney, Jesse Bertron, Rita Bullwinkel, Mary Somerville, Max McDonough, Kelsey Norris and the rest of my loving Vanderbilt MFA cohort, and the thriving Nashville literary community for the immeasurable encouragement, advice, and inspiration.

Special thanks to my family—Bill Brown, endless gratitude to my dearest teacher, to Ryan Clark, you are my one, Alex Kanski, my sister always, and most of all to my courageous mother, Verna Knight, this book is for you.

CONTENTS

There is always a road,
The sea, dark hair, dolor.

Always a question
Bigger than itself—

—Tracy K. Smith

EQUILIBRIUM

Took me   thirty years to say
I'm glad   I don't pass for white.
Pressed   those words into the dark
creases   in my palm like a fortune:
a life line   of futures I wanted to begin.
Like the way   the haze of summer heat
makes   a drive home different.
Right now   even the streetlights
have a misty   orb to them. Even
the cigarette butt   flicked out
of the window   on the highway
plumes with embers   skidding
toward me   like the tail
of a backyard   bottle rocket.
I wanted my   hair straighter,
nose thinner,   skin lighter.
I thought this   is what my white
boyfriends   wanted as their hands
became   each European request,
a Russian   nesting doll I kept
un-stacking   until there was only illusion
of beauty   split open. Like the Great
Gatsby cover   with the disembodied head
of a crying   flapper over the neon-scape
of city. All   the green beacons we chase
as thoughts   of people who don't love us
are left back   drifting on the roads as we
drive. But   every muscle knows how
to get home.   How the smallest part
of ourselves   cannot be divided.
The last doll   is still whole in my hands.
Even the car   can still purr from energy
after it's been   turned off. What is left
whispering   in us, once we have
stopped trying   to become the other?

THE FREQUENCY OF GOODNIGHT

The duende is not in the throat:
the duende surges up, inside,
from the soles of the feet.
—Federico García Lorca

Like so many nights of my childhood
I lived inside the fishbowl
of a one-bedroom apartment,
    waited for my mother to come home
    (from her second job). As a waitress
    she wore orthopedic shoes for flat feet.
All her uniforms blur together: IHOP,
    Red Lobster, Rainforest Café, Shoney's...
This is how she tucked me in—
    jingle and clack of keys
would turn the doorknob open
    allow me to fall asleep.
She tucked me in— not with blankets
    or a kiss on the forehead,
but with locking the door behind her.
    My single mother would take those big,
boxy shoes off, unhook her bra
    (too tired to take it all the way off)
and eat the leftover pizza
    I had ordered for dinner.
Television shadows flickered
    her exhausted frame, smell
of other people's food on her skin,
    crumpled ones, fives, and tens
fanned out of her server book.
    I heard the change from bad tippers
like hail on the kitchen counter.
    Maybe for other children

the purr of the air conditioner, the sound
  of a ceiling fan whisking the darkness,
or the steady neon glow of a nightlight
  set their dreams ablaze?
But for me, hearing those keys
  slipped me under the wing
of my mother's white noise.

Let me begin again,
  when I was a waitress during college,
I had the shoes that doctors and nurses
  wore to support their posture.
Saturdays I worked doubles,
  toward the end of my two shifts
my pace would slow—
  as I made laps around my tables,
picked up half eaten sandwiches,
  grabbed wadded napkins with chewed
gristle. When we closed,
  I'd be on my hands and knees,
as I swept litter from the day,
  collected broken-off ends of French fries,
dislodged pucks of used gum,
  dragged swollen and leaky trash bags
to the dumpster.
  Bone heavy and body tired—
I would come home,
  take those heavy wooden clogs off.
Turn on some show and listen
  to the cadence of dialogue
like a metronome tipping my head
  to the baptism of sleep.

Let me begin again,
  The first dead body I ever saw
was my grandmother. Alzheimer's—
  My mother said, *She always left*
  that old TV on while she slept...
    damn frequencies messed with her head.
If I focus now, I can still see my mom
  asleep in her uniform on the couch—
feet propped up, open pizza box
  dappled in grease stains.
I would tiptoe and turn off the television,
  slink back to our bedroom.
This is how I tucked her in.
  This is how we said goodnight.

HAIR RELAXER: AN ORIGIN STORY

...never to look a hot comb in the teeth.
—Gwendolyn Brooks

You came into this world, creamy—full of alkali and burn,
like a baby born of hard labor. Ruler of all things straight
and acceptable. You made kinky your nemesis, fought

genetic bend of curls. Cold lotions brush-stroked the Afro
on our heads inside of our hearts to bloom. Wait for it...
scratch of matchsticks ignited on the scalp. Wait for it...

sting of water pressure on the fleshy bottom of new scabs.
I was seven when it first happened to me. Told mama,
I wanted my hair to swing like the white girls in my school!

I cried at the shampoo bowl, thought pain would make me
beautiful. Learned to suck it up, keep it in, tucked and folded
like origami. Blow dryer wiped those tears away. Salon girl

said, *Ohhh, we got it so straight this time!* Singe, on the teeth
of a hot comb forged from the European Gods of smooth metal.
Swipe from root to unruly tip. Rise of smoke—from the kindling

of burnt black hair. Rise of smoke—smogging the salons and
kitchens from coarse-haired daughters and mothers. Rise of smoke—
from the altar of our vanity. All the wavy hair I broke like the back

of a slave into submission, into black yarn I knew inside me grew
to find my way out of this chemical labyrinth. Out of wanting boys
to glide their wanting hands through my straight hair, out of my

own Minotaur of self-hatred, but I slayed the beast of pretty!
Took my hair inch by inch like the yarn of Theseus to find my
way back to my little self, back to my baby pictures with a fro-pik

in my hair, to the bounce, the spring in every coil. Rain, I am not
afraid of you. Let the water take me back to curls. Let the water
be gospel, brown hydrangea, my grandmother's silver cotton boll,

my auntie's cornrows, my mother's hands kneading almond oil
in my scalp like coating a cast iron pan to shiny black patina. I came
into this world greasy, full of thick psalms. Let the water take me back.

MAGIC

Light as a feather stiff as a board, light as a feather stiff as a board,
we chanted as children. We believed we could levitate bodies with
our words. Like in my church, when the preacher placed charismatic

fire in the palm of his hands to the crucible of our foreheads. He would
shout *Jesus!* Blow peppermint-scented breath of Spirit on each face.
The huddled congregation fell like drunken dominoes around the altar,

wriggling on the swivel of spiritual intoxication. They called it
slain in the spirit, consumed by divine ecstasy. I wanted to be the
next ember, feel the singe from God all over my body, except when

the preacher laid his hands on me—I felt nothing, only the dry
heat of his dragon mouth. I wanted to believe their version of Jesus
wouldn't skip me. So when he tried again, pushing me to a slant—

I gave in. Lying on the carpet, encircled by hysterical laughter and
blissed out faces I cried—I was pretending. Same with the child
chants, Bloody Mary was never in the mirror, and the Ouija boards—

I felt nothing, just fingers guiding toward letters with no message for me.
How we fake to feel the magic inside us. It took me a while to understand
that I didn't have to beg for it. God was already washing the dust off my feet.

BLACK CHAMPAGNE

I sing God's music because it makes me feel free.
—Mahalia Jackson

Mother shimmers when she sings in the choir—
rowing in the sway of satin robes thick with gospel music.

Smooth & forgiving when her mouth spills godly notes
& Fashion Fair-lipped hymns. She towers over the back

row of sopranos—tall, a braided palm tree with un-fisted
fingers held high in praise. But in seconds—her song

could pitch in the key of shouting. So guttural, like tiny
shovels digging up the body's gravel after midnight—

when she comes home from her third job to my undone
chores & rips the bi-fold laundry doors off the metal tracks

& hurls them at me yelling: *I asked you to do one thing!*
One thing like an echo… Same as when the Holy Ghost

kidnaps the sanctuary—lapping steam from the pews with
a slurp & the music leader starts twitching his head & hands.

It's about to rumble through & the building is shaking too
as the choir jerks & hollers, bends & snaps back their spines

to surging piano glissandos—a stampede of *touched* men
& women buck their silky bodies as the church steams

tropical with tired breath. But after the service, mother
is crying again, dripping mascara over my face—warm

trickle of communion as she spanks the taut tambourine
of my young body to beat inside her 2/4 clapping, a ballad

to purge all that black champagne. Something about dirty
dishes in the sink again, about her waxy palms cracking holy

thunderheads on my skin—bruising something I do not know
how to name between us, except for the hymn she is humming.

I know this song.

THE SPOT IN ANTIOCH

And he that sitteth on [any] thing whereon he sat that hath
the issue shall wash his clothes, and bathe himself in water,
and be unclean until the even.
— Leviticus 15:5

                              Oh they came, they came from our church,
a surprise. We didn't know, how could we? We didn't know how poor
we were until the lovely, sugar-fresh ladies came to our one-bedroom
apartment, on the duskier side of town. *Knock, Knock, Knock!*

                              Through the cloudy peephole—
busking upturned brooms and twirling yellow gloves like rubber daises,
plastic buckets, spongy sponges and bleach, so much white white bleach
to clean our home, because they could, because my mother let them in.

We are blessing you! You work so hard and you are all alone, we are
the Christian Cleaning Brigade! You are a single mother, oh we pity,
let us clean, let us clean, they said—a singing choir to the least of these.

                              They started dusting and sweeping and sorting—
Oh, where does this go? Is this trash? Is this trash? they chanted.
Opened closets, fingered our clothes and dishes, *swish-clank-shut.*
Our apartment was theirs. We, the strangers, brown bugs scattering
to edge the dusty baseboards with our shrinking bodies—got out of their way.

Where's your vacuum, dear? Oh, it's so old, my mother had one just like this.
The bright crucifix dangling over creamy clavicles like a pure silver bullet
swaying over the bathtub, a pendulum ticking and tocking the ceramic lip,
while milk-blue powder christened every mushroom-colored ring.

                              They made it snow.

And their makeup was porcelain perfect, too.
Plum-dark lip liner traced vermillion borders
as they smiled, they never stopped smiling—

until they found it, behind the toilet like a lurch. I forgot I left it there.
One lady came out with my stained underwear, holding it up and away
from her body like a stench. My period bruising the pearly cotton with
a smear of red poppies. My horror, my ooze, my face—

I was the adulteress caught
naked in the streets in front of Jesus. Their unsmiling, stone faces
seeing my midras, my unclean spot before them.
The way they slashed their guillotine eyes at my fresh body—
to have had so much blood in me like a dirty, new sin.

EXORCISM

Pastor John stood over her body,
shouted scripture as she writhed in the jerk
of undulations that lit her bones on fire. Her eyes
slick as marbles slid to the back of her head. Only
the white jelly of sclera shone between the flutter
of eyelash flicks moored to the mouth of some
netherworld. I stood back in awe and in horror
like the first time I watched porn. Excited, because
we were inside the same heat as each of our hands
stretched forward, flexed as church fans we stroked
the flames of spirit higher and higher. She frothed
her lips to a disc of crema, cried and whimpered
almost like a self-soothing baby. Our finger pads
followed the bars on the pages of a hymnal book.
My youth group spoke as a choir in tongues, our
syllabic utterings were plucked marionette strings
that pulled her limbs to spasms. Pastor John said
she had a demon of lust, a *Jezebel Spirit*. He said
we had to pray louder and harder, had to touch her
arms and her sides, had to deliver the ember of her
sins from the second crust of hell. But I knew this
girl that twitched on the floor. Sarah, my older friend.
And yes, she made out with boys. And yes, I saw
how the boys looked at her breasts, like the way
they looked at them now when she jiggled, buoyant
as sunny side up eggs. As if I could pierce her yolks
with my praying fingers, bloodletting buttery sex.
She was like me: a girl with no father, a girl that
made God her father, a girl that wanted to be saved,
but mostly to be loved. She gave her body to greasy
boys—the way she gave her body, in that musty chapel
outside of the gold buckle of the Bible Belt, to all of us.

A PSALM FOR THE ONE

O taste & see David's lips,

      his mouth: a crucifix for my wet begging.

When he sang worship songs—

     I emptied my pockets, my purse,
& let down my hair for a tenth of his blue gaze.

The Lord said *He was The One*,

    so church girls bought wedding dresses.

O to be saved by a man who could sing like that—
    slippery vocal runs
      warm on fingertips melting sin.

I never sought to be like the stupid girls

     but when he grabbed my crotch, I said—*Yes*.
An altar for his drossy hands was my body.

I became the Easter poinsettias too,
    open & red, shiny with lacquer.

Yes to curry that laced our tongues with yellow spice.
    We laid in bed & burped & laughed all night.

We saw a couple having sex in a car.
    He stayed & watched as they watched him.

I held his hand on the streets walking home,
    thought I heard a voice say *He is The One*, but—

the summer wind can mimic almost any wish.

A grown man crying in my car—
A grown man picking a speck of black pepper
from the wet groove of my gums with a toothpick

like wheedling a soft prayer. Amen.

He almost destroyed New York,
but I didn't want New York anyway.
Amen.

How every tug & tough was a bite that drew no blood.
Amen.

The last email said I was just
a really good friend... a sister in Christ.
Amen.

We slowly gnawed at the savior of desire,

a valley of dry humping
that made raw heat but no spark. Selah.

& when he wasn't singing I was lying
with my body.

& when there was no more milk—
I left him,

but in some ways
I am still walking down this aisle on my knees.

A BLUE NOTE FOR FATHER'S DAY

Because I don't know where you are—
I send you a letter of tree leaves

I heard this morning harmonizing
like emerald waves above a pond.

I send you John Coltrane,
who locked himself in a room of amethyst

for days with no food or mercy to write
A Love Supreme.

We destroy ourselves for splendor—
emerging from the buried deep

like cicada song to mate & disappear again.
Today, I will not be bitter

about this holiday or the Facebook posts.
No, today I send you a roofless church,

a grotto with fuzzy moss & trickling water
that sounds like wet piano keys.

Please know—I've made good with my life.
With or without you, I know how to kneel

before imperfect men. I know this pond can carry
cold morning skin like blue blue notes

pressed from warm saxophone buttons for:
Acknowledgment, Resolution, Pursuance & Psalm.

Dear father, I hope you know that I can love
the absence of a thing even more than

the thing itself. That I can have one day a year
that doesn't beat like the rest.

& friends, don't ever wish to be me.
You don't want this sunless song.

There is no number in my phone to call.
There is no home with his face I remember,

just a place called Nowhere & this is where
I find & lose him like a savior.

TRIPTYCH FOR MY FATHER

*

Inside a Burbank hospital, my mother lies in a room full of people fixed to the bright oculus on her stomach—but a room can become so many things at once. Even with nurses scurrying around the hive of her body, this woman was alone with her breath, holding her own hands. I did not fit the natural way, so they cut me into this world. A ten-pound creamy baby. My mother's middle folded into layers of brown watermelon skin (that she will later flash at random to show how my entrance made a ruin of her figure). The first thing I want to remember is her chocolate head. What did she find in my body to claim first: my nose, my mouth? I was all hers for that brief moment when I was only her last name.

*

My mother retells the story in so many different ways that my father is myth, an absent god, but a God. A twenty-year-old with shaggy brown hair and scarlet pimples from the sheen of slippery butter where they worked at the Hollywood Bowl's popcorn stand. *She says* she called, but he couldn't find a ride to the hospital. *She says* they weren't even talking by then. *She says* they were together. *No*, they were broken up. *No*, they were broken up, but living together. A relationship can become so many things at once. The truth is I have his eyes.

*

A church girl told me, *You know you can ask God for anything, just like your real dad!* I squinched—my eyes—two plump grapes to burst and prayed my requests as if I was flipping a silver coin into the clear hands of heaven and wishing for *heads–heads–heads*, but prayer can become so many things at once like a syllogism: All men are mortal. My father is a man. Therefore, my father is mortal. *Our birth is but a sleep and a*
                                                                    forgetting.

FLAMBEAUX

Tipsy, I am, in Louisiana among the throng of loose bodies lit
by the liquid flame of flambeaux— fiery torches foreshadowing
my night to unfurl. My arms like the arms of black men carrying
heavy torches, and before them, the wet limbs of shiny slaves lighting white
pleasures of dark men floating in the deep throat of night. I stay with my
friends at first, but I fall into a cab with some frat guys. One
of them says, *For a kiss, baby,* *I'll take you to the French Quarter.*
My lips were on his and our scissoring mouths ignite my descent down
to Bourbon Street. Enveloped, I am, in the murmuration of Mardi Gras
with a thousand buzzing bee bodies dancing and rubbing in fixed figure
eights trying to sway one inch in all directions, but all of us are stuck
in each other's movements above the sludge of wet black trash
around my feet, as anonymous hands grab my crotch. I am going
to die inside the muscled swallow of a crowd's grip. I tell you it's
only the older ripened women who show off their tits. The crowd
spits me up like Jonah at the beach of McDonald's. I run into my friends
again, eat some French fries and lick the tiny salt granules off the tips
of my finger pads. They want to dance to black music, but not with
black people. So I ditch them again, and find the reason I came
down to this orgy machine in the first place—my ex-boyfriend.
He is here, somewhere in the grind of the city's slick engine, and through
cryptic texts and loud phone calls of us shouting our coordinates over loud
music we find each other at the dark corner of some dive bar, heat-seeking
missiles ready to destroy. We were on the high floor
of his hotel room with booming war drums of bacchanalia below—
cigarette ash in my hair like dirty glitter, sticky liquor and the sweat
of the street still on our skin. The boiling breath of flambeaux
still on my charcoal body, an ember that never left me as the starless
night burst below—glowing fire tongues in the obsidian stew lick
sodden faces of Flambeaux men and women in processional,
laughing and hollering for dollars and flickering coins—the pulsing
middle of the luminous parade, pumping kerosene over their heads—
a volcanic wonder. A gorgeous lava spilling down my lips, our fingernails

filthy with each other and powdered
and gators and gumbo in my teeth,
purples, golds, and greens whizzing
but the whole city fills my mouth,
throat to inferno, inside of me—
stirring underworld, flame-woven
percolating. Phlegethon,

sugar from greasy beignets, hot sauce
metallic beads: a blur of flashing
in the air. A royal feast it is, not him,
swallowing down my dazzling
thick wicks dipped in wax, the
with gagging delight—
what a river of blood I am.

TELL ME: HARLEM

Every day, I walked over the ashes of Langston Hughes
    & his glittering cosmogram of ancient rivers,
    stepped over the dancing feet of Maya & Baraka
    that summer at The Schomburg,
I sifted through newspaper reels like a slot machine junkie
    & on my way home
    read the braille of black gum
    on the sidewalk saying—*No, this is renaissance!*
But my mind was fixed on your footnotes.
    Yes, my mind was lit
    by the hot strips of my first Brazilian wax.
    My lust I carried up & down 135th like a throbbing beast.
Every breeze was a subway surging
    through my new bare body as I walked by splayed
    papayas with shiny dark seeds & fuzzy kiwis
    with nuclear green flesh.
A man shoved bruised roses in my face,
    Fresh flowers for you!
    A man in a sharp suit preached Nation of Islam.
    Bustelo coffee with blossoming cream
& everything bagels with sesames stuck in my teeth.
    Don't forget extra schmear!
    & steaming manhole covers simmering below
    LED billboards as brilliant as the neon sun.
The New York Times in Russian,
    Spanish r's trilling like a deck of cards—
    wafts of warm piss & baked curb trash.
    Yes, the city was ripe & found every opening
in my body to enter. Taxis zoomed
    by as the earth gusted my puffed pores.
    Oh, the tortuous mating rituals!
    My naked center ripped the burning city raw

& I bit down on every crisp and living thing.
I was smashed, a stranger—
sizzling in lavish multitudes,
my lips gnashed, tore through day & night.
Harlem, tell me, we carried each other.
Tell me, I meant something.
Tell me, you remember sucking
barbeque sauce off my fingers.
Didn't every moment seem sticky
& weren't we always eating?
Tell me, I own one of your Fourth of Julys.
Tell me, Mexican street corn
was our whole summer.
Tell me, hot mayonnaise & Cotija
danced in our mouths
the last time I held your gaze.

PARTICLE FEVER

They built a seventeen-mile circle
to recreate the big bang,
how the laws of physics crash

like a drum beat of what makes us.
Your hand finding mine in the car ride home,
as white lines on the highway blur into memory.

I do not need to know every answer.
Give me a plane ride to question my ego.
When you are mad,

give me my first name in your mouth—
hard consonant of *T,*
said with the Tip of the Tongue.

What we speak into existence
like a drum beat of what makes us.
Give me a plane ride to question myself.

Aren't we always flying,
into each other
into the mouth of the universe?

Could it be magic?
The white bunny we lift from the hat
like early fog on the road to work.

We discover foot by foot
how we grope for each other,
sway to music we don't even hear.

There is always movement—
atoms bouncing around us
like a room full of endless balloons.

The seen and unseen world.
What wanted to be born out of nothing?
Mouth open—kiss ready:

lit with charge and wonder.

BROKEN GHAZAL FOR WALTER SCOTT

*You can't write poems about the trees when the woods are full of
policemen.*

—Bertolt Brecht

A video looping like a dirge on repeat, my soul—a psalm of bullets in my back.
I see you running then drop heavy hunted like prey with eight shots in the back.

Again, in my Facebook feed another black man dead, another fist in my throat.
You: prostrate on the green grass with handcuffed hands on your bleeding back.

Praises for the video, to the witness & his recording thumb, praises to YouTube
for taking the blindfold off Lady Justice, dipping her scales down with old weight

of strange fruit, to American eyeballs blinking & chewing the 24-hour news cycle:
another black body, another white cop. But let us go back to the broken tail light,

let's find a man behind on his child support, let's become his children, let's call
him *Papa.* Let us chant *Papa, don't run! Stay, stay back! Stay here with us.* But Tiana—

you have got to stop watching this video. Walter is gone & he is not your daddy,
another story will come to your feed, stay back. But whisper—*stay,* once more,

with the denied breath of his absent CPR, praise his mother strumming Santana
with tiny *hallelujahs* up & down the harp of his back. Praise his mother holding

the man who made her son a viral hit, a rerun to watch him die *ad infinitum,* again
we go back, click replay at any moment. A video looping like a dirge on repeat—

SANDY SPEAKS

Because I did not turn my signal on for Death –

Sandy speaks to me
beyond her grave
her voice on YouTube—
    ricochets.

He harshly stopped for me –

The body is gone
& the words remain
she says,
You can't tell me God ain't good.
& I want to believe her
but how did she die
    & when did the murdering start?

The police car held but just Ourselves –

So many questions
she cannot answer
& They will not answer
but she testifies in Death.
She says again,
You can't tell me God ain't good
& I want to believe her.
I am a black woman, too—
I fasten my seatbelt—
I check the speed limit—
push the needle to hover
just under 30 mph.
I click the turn signal in my car
    & say her name.

Immortality.

HOW TO FIND THE CENTER OF A CIRCLE

Of all the things that happened there
That's all that I remember.
　　　　　　—Countee Cullen, "Incident"

$(x)^2$	$+ (y)^2$	$= r^2$
The first time	I	was called a *nigger*
with those	red hot	*g* sounds,
molten syllables	as searing lassos	around my neck
at a skating rink	they	like white spiders
spun around me	silking	a carousel of hate.
I didn't know	what	the word meant
but my body	blackened	wrong with heat.
Ugly	marked	a radius of shameful skin
as two white boys	taunted me	on roller skates,
they curved	the loop of	my circumference. I was
a little girl	crying	in the center of a circle—
felt	my selves	begin to double.
How	did I know	I was different?
I told the teacher	and she	put them in timeout.
But what about	the little girl	rolling away, struck
with the red	hot *g* sounds	ringing fire songs
in her ears?	You never forget	the first time
you are branded	with iron—	seared raw, permanent.

BEAR WITNESS

after Carrie Mae Weems's Roaming *series*

Before I knew
how to fill my onyx body
with slick measures,

dip every curve
in my skin with dark sway,
I needed a picture.

Before me stood
a long black dress I called *Woman*—
you stand opaque

with your back to me,
a statue of witness,
the door of Yes—

I can Return
to the monument
of your silhouette

to find my longest muscle.
We both stare down
the ocean to stillness.

O, Carrie—
what are you trying
to tell me here?

I've been standing by water
my whole damn life
trying to get saved.

WAKING IN THE VANDERBILT PSYCHIATRIC HOSPITAL

Spring, 2004

I watch the students come and go
through my gold and black window,

bright indigo of daylight sluicing through
dark boundaries on my skin hue
(I was black, so black I was blue).

Locked—in spotted eggshell cage,
like vanilla/black bean speckled crème brûlée.
My tiny spoon goes: *tap-tap-crack.*

Creamy pills, pills three times a day,
anesthetic, floating stone—
a nurse siphons daily communion

from my pinot-bright DNA.
But, I see myself in a dazzling dream,
while the interlocutor says to me,

You've got so many daddies
from West End to Jefferson Street!
My pattering heart filled with Jubilee singing

double-dutch ropes cut me in half
like splayed grapefruit pink topaz—
two Tianas live in Nashville now.

The Parthenon lies just in between
my mom and dad's histories.
Du Bois digs me plain at TSU

but the Fugitives have pooled
my *other* tears to flood blue.
Tate fire breathes with brackish might

sugar burn my lips to caramelize
or sip me Sunday morning cool,
a greyhound with Confederate-dead

clinking ice. Drink me, eat me,
wash me clinical and white.
I'm trying recall the poem Langston

wrote how heavy Harlem sags,
my dream to poet—
Does it stink like rotten meat?

A middle passage inside of me,
black bodies from the ballast cries—
ocean spray into funeral-speak,

every inky pen I pick up bleeds.
I want to write a happy word,
but every line jazzes elegy.

It does not matter what wild honey
drove me here for dark angels to sing:
I'm all Bessie, Billy, and Simone—

black pain swinging, sweet and low.
On this sill—I see my prism fate
through golden yolk of sun,

one day I will get out of here
and find my future had begun.

BNA → LAX

I return to my birthplace with a focus on breath.
It's easier to inhale the California landscape.

In Tennessee, I live in a bowl of green suffocation—
hillsides consume & stack with bouquets of trees.

I'm at the bottom wanting to look up & over, yet
driving through the Mojave desert is smoker's teeth—

expansive shades of yellow rust, Suessical Joshua trees,
mountain range in the distance followed by cracked

sea floor. The bluest skyline traces the face of the earth
for miles as I drive. Now, I know I come from clutter

& hoarding, like the makeup & Q-tips that litter my
bathroom counter in constellations of chaos. I come

from single mothers with big pores like black pepper
on my nose. I come from Pacoima United Methodist

Church, from older black ladies remembering my
grandmother & my mother & me as a little girl,

hugging my neck with compliments as Hawaiian leis,
saying *how pretty & all grown up* I am, saying they

remember me running through the pews with frilly,
white socks, telling me to bring some sunshine back

home. But in Nashville—the weather is bipolar & I'm
always the black thumb. I found my meditation on

the Venice boardwalk. Hadn't been on a bike in years.
Wobbled through break boys, whiffs of dank marijuana,

Chihuahuas & pit bulls on leashes, drum circles
with dancing transients, wet graffiti on concrete,

sweet cut from a fresh mango cart with juice dripping
down her hands, denim on denim and no one cared

the color of my husband's hand holding mine.
Somewhere in Laguna, I wrote my name by the lip

of the ocean. I come from breaking beach waves with
the sand sucking the detritus from the center of the earth.

PROMETHEIA REMIXED

POWER
We've reached the end of the road, the topmost stone on the rooftop
of the world.

FORCE
Beyond here, everything is downhill.
—Robert Lowell

1. Bound

I summon the fire bringer
on refrain, a medium rare liver steak
shredded by the eager beak
of a black pen scrawling the skin of a page.

Yes, yes the *Promethean* heat, stolen fire
liquid me. Each prompt digging secret pain
—carry me. Mommy me. *When I was a child*,
Saint Paul said, first the milk and then the meat.

I am chained to the rock till I become the rock,
heavy metal shackles dangle around my feet.
Rip the white Daddy poems out of me:

You do not do, you do not do
Any more, black shoe
you are the greedy beak.

2. Unbound

Mixed Bitch is allowed to love herself.
Mixed Bitch lets herself love—
the black inside: the white inside: the black of herself.

She wants to tell Nikky Finney
about her *beautiful black girl arms*
how they shimmer and shimmy in space—
making muscle songs of tendons and the dark matter beef.

Mixed Bitch wants to commission Kehinde Wiley.
She wants renaissance prints behind her mulatto skin,
gold lamé and a big ass frame inside the Frist Museum.

She was caught between two allegiances, different,
yet the same. Herself. Her race. Race! The thing
that bound and suffocated her. Whatever steps
she took, or if she took none at all,
something would be crushed. Crushed?

Mixed Bitch don't know her Daddy.
Mixed Bitch don't know her Daddy.
Mixed   Bitch
      don't   know
her   Daddy.

3. Origin

The bright chains
Eat with their burning cold into my bones.
Heaven's wingèd hound, polluting from thy lips
His beak in poison not his own, tears up
My heart.

Yes, yes I hear that handsome bird screech for me.
Every day,
I keep writing about the same new scar—
begging to close
on my fresh belly and every day
I welcome the first bite.

Open every cabinet inside myself uncluttered.
Take it. He takes me in his mouth like war.

Gorgeous fluid slashes out—red lace,
endless red lace spills down the mountain
of memory. Mom is Dad :: Dad is Mom.

White Dad is the Eagle hunting me,
taking my Body as communion.
I am the Wine and Bread of slavery.
White Dad is the Eagle preying on me.

Warm butter was my mother.
Dad likes otherness on toast
like he likes his black women:
spread and melting and greasy.

Black Mom, wanting so badly
to be consumed by a white man,
for a white man to make her French
toast from the inside-out.

Their differences smashing into each other,
skin engines of self-hatred that made me.

The ruling principle of Hate,
Which for its pleasure doth create
The things it may annihilate.

4. The Fire-Bringer

We are so civilized
and because of this the tribes of men upon earth burn
white bones to the deathless gods upon fragrant altars.

I wish I could have seen Paul Robeson play Othello—

                              His large
wingspan thick with oily feathers deep
in Laconian black and subterranean tenor boom.

I want to see him smother
a white woman
on stage every night and every night

after the play
make love to that same
pure milk he loved so much that hates

his buzzing blight.
Paul, push that prop pillow
through her porcelain face

till the force of power shatters
tiny bones to craquelure glaze.
Yes, yes the eggshell crunch,

tiny neck bones of black men, dead
weight swinging from the immortal limbs
of lynching trees—seven cervical vertebrae

snap like surrounding twigs in the throat.
The top bone is called the Atlas, another
punishment. Enduring the knot, holding

the earth and heavens apart. The body
slackens, gorgeous head slumps downward
in the way Paul dipped down
                              toward Peggy

Ashcroft as Desdemona—
Look to her, Moor, if thou hast eyes to see.
She hath deceived her father and may thee.

The safe word is safe.
The safe word is torment.
The safe word is thief.

Crack the interracial craving before it cracks you.
Beige makeup on the pillow every night—
creamy Rorschach test, muffled mascara

and red lipstick inkblots. From the dream,
we wake, take the black bird by its quill,
dip in swaying slave ship darkness—
                              Let freedom bleed.

NOTES

"The Frequency of Goodnight" is after Terrance Hayes's poem "The Same City."

"Black Champagne" is after Robert Hayden's poem "The Whipping."

"The Spot in Antioch" is after Gwendolyn Brooks's poem "The Lovers of the Poor."

"Sandy Speaks" is after Emily Dickinson's poem "Because I could not stop for Death (479)."

"Triptych for my Father" ends with a line from William Wordsworth's poem "Ode on Intimations of Immortality from Recollections of Early Childhood."

"*Particle Fever*" shares its title with the documentary film *Particle Fever*, directed by Mark Levinson, 2013.

"Waking in the Vanderbilt Psychiatric Hospital" is after Robert Lowell's poem "Waking in the Blue." The line, "Does it stink like rotten meat?" is borrowed from Langston Hughes's poem "Harlem."

"Prometheia Remixed" is after Robert Duncan's poem "Osiris and Set." Lines in the poem are taken from these various texts:

> Epigraph
> Robert Lowell, "Prometheus Bound"

> "Promethean heat"
> William Shakespeare, *Othello*

> "When I was a child…"
> Johann Wolfgang von Goethe, "Prometheus"
> in reference to 1 Corinthians 13:11 from Saint Paul.

"You do not do, you do not do
Any more, black shoe"
    Sylvia Plath, "Daddy"

The reference to Nikky Finney is after her speech, "A Young
Black Woman Shimmy & Shakes a Flagpole and Finally
Brings the Confederate Flag Down After One Hundred Years:
Thoughts on Climbing, Not Waiting on the Calvary, Faith, and
Manners, in the Contemporary South."

"She was caught between two allegiances, different, yet the
same. Herself. Her race. Race! The thing that bound and
suffocated her. Whatever steps she took, or if she took none at
all, something would be crushed."
    Nella Larson, *Passing* (1929)

"The bright chains
Eat with their burning cold into my bones.
Heaven's wingèd hound, polluting from thy lips
His beak in poison not his own, tears up
My heart."
    Percy Bysshe Shelley, "Prometheus Unbound"

"The ruling principle of Hate,
Which for its pleasure doth create
The things it may annihilate."
    Lord Byron, "Prometheus"

"and because of this the tribes of men upon earth burn
white bones to the deathless gods upon fragrant altars."
    Hesiod, "Theogony"

"Look to her, Moor, if thou hast eyes to see.
She hath deceived her father and may thee."
    William Shakespeare, *Othello*

ABOUT THE AUTHOR

photo by Crystal K. Martel

TIANA CLARK is the winner of the 2016 Academy of American Poets Prize and the 2015 *Rattle* Poetry Prize. She is currently an MFA candidate at Vanderbilt University where she serves as the Poetry Editor for *Nashville Review*. Tiana has received scholarships to The Sewanee Writers' Conference and The New Harmony Writers Workshop. Her writing has appeared in or is forthcoming from *Best New Poets 2015*, *Crab Orchard Review*, *Southern Indiana Review*, *The Adroit Journal*, *Muzzle Magazine*, *Thrush*, *The Offing*, and elsewhere. Find her online at www.tianaclark.com.

About

THE FROST PLACE
CHAPBOOK COMPETITION

The Frost Place is a nonprofit educational center for poetry and the arts based at Robert Frost's old homestead, which is owned by the Town of Franconia, New Hampshire. In 1976, a group of Franconia residents, led by David Schaffer and Evangeline Machlin, persuaded the Franconia town meeting to approve the purchase of the farmhouse where Robert Frost and his family lived full-time from 1915 to 1920 and spent nineteen summers. A board of trustees was given responsibility for management of the house and its associated programs, which now include several conferences and seminars, readings, a museum located in the Frost farmhouse, and yearly fellowships for emerging American poets.

The Frost Place Chapbook Competition awards an annual prize to a chapbook of poems. In addition to publication of the collection by Bull City Press, the winning author receives a fellowship to The Frost Place Poetry Seminar, a cash prize, and week-long residency to live and write in The Frost Place farmhouse.

2016   Tiana Clark, *Equilibrium*
        SELECTED BY AFAA MICHAEL WEAVER

2015   Anders Carlson-Wee, *Dynamite*
        SELECTED BY JENNIFER GROTZ

2014   Lisa Gluskin Stonestreet, *The Greenhouse*
        SELECTED BY DAVID BAKER

2013   Jill Osier, *Should Our Undoing Come Down Upon Us White*
        SELECTED BY PATRICK DONNELLY

ALSO FROM BULL CITY PRESS

LENA BERTONE
Behind This Mirror

KATIE BOWLER
State Street

ELLEN C. BUSH
Licorice

BEN HOFFMAN
Together, Apart

ANNE KEEFE
Lithopedia

MICHAEL MARTONE
Memoranda

MICHAEL McFEE
The Smallest Talk

EMILIA PHILLIPS
Beneath the Ice Fish Like Souls Look Alike

ANNA ROSS
Figuring

ANNE VALENTE
An Elegy for Mathematics

LAURA VAN DEN BERG
There Will Be No More Good Nights Without Good Nights

MATTHEW OLZMANN & ROSS WHITE, eds.
Another & Another:
An Anthology from the Grind Daily Writing Series